SAUCES & SALSAS
◆ FOR THE GRILL ◆

Creative Cooking Library

By the Editors of Sunset Books

SUNSET BOOKS

President & Publisher: Susan J. Maruyama
Director, Finance & Business Affairs: Gary Loebner
**Director, Manufacturing
& Sales Service:** Lorinda Reichert
Director, Sales & Marketing: Richard A. Smeby
Director, New Business: Kenneth Winchester
Editorial Director: Bob Doyle
Developmental Editor: Lynne Gilberg

SUNSET PUBLISHING CORPORATION

Chairman: Jim Nelson
President/Chief Executive Officer: Robin Wolaner
Chief Financial Officer: James E. Mitchell
Publisher: Stephen J. Seabolt
Circulation Director: Robert I. Gursha
Editor, Sunset Magazine: William R. Marken
Senior Editor, Food & Entertaining: Jerry Anne Di Vecchio

All the recipes in this book were developed and tested in the Sunset test kitchens. For information about any Sunset Book please call 1-800-634-3095.

The nutritional data provided for each recipe is for a single serving, based on the number of servings and the amount of each ingredient. If a range is given for the number of servings and/or the amount of an ingredient, the analysis is based on the average of the figures given. The nutritional analysis does not include optional ingredients or those for which no specific amount is stated. If an ingredient is listed with a substitution, the data was calculated using the first choice.

Nutritional analysis of recipes: Hill Nutrition Associates, Inc. of Florida.

Sunset Creative Cooking Library
was produced by St. Remy Press

President: Pierre Léveillé
Managing Editor: Carolyn Jackson
Managing Art Director: Diane Denoncourt
Senior Editor: Elizabeth Cameron
Art Director: Chantal Bilodeau
Editorial Assistant: Jennifer Meltzer
Administrator: Natalie Watanabe
Production Manager: Michelle Turbide
System Coordinator: Éric Beaulieu
Proofreader: Veronica Schami
Indexer: Christine Jacobs

The following persons also assisted in the preparation of this book: Philippe Arnoldi, Maryse Doray, Lorraine Doré, Dominique Gagné, Geneviève Monette.

COVER: Cranberry Salsa (page 47)

PHOTOGRAPHY
Peter Christiansen: 26, 28, 32, 42, 56; Deborah Jones: 50; Norman A. Plate: 4, 20, 40, 52; Darrow M. Watt: Inside cover, 3, 5, 6, 24, 30, 34; Tom Wyatt: Cover, 16, 46, 60; Nikolay Zurek: 7, 12, 36; 48.

ISBN 0-376-00907-1
Library of Congress Catalog Card Number 94-069956
Printed in the United States.

♻ printed on recycled paper

Table of Contents

Getting Started

Red tomatoes or tart green tomatillos determine the color of sauces and salsas; chiles imbue heat.

Many a backyard chef has built a reputation on deftly seasoned condiments. The recipes in this book range from spicy and slightly sweet barbecue sauces to fiery-hot salsas that rely on chiles to add heat. The fresh and dried chiles shown on page 7 are a sampling of the hundreds of mild to hot varieties. Use the photographs for identification when purchasing chiles.

Barbecue cooks also are rediscovering relishes and chutneys, some made with pomegranates, cranberries, papayas, and pineapples to lend an exotic flavor to a range of grilled foods. The fruits, blended with fresh ginger, nutmeg, cumin, and a variety of spices conjure up the taste and tradition of the East.

Safety Information

It is unsafe to use aluminum bowls to mix ingredients for sauces, salsas, relishes, and chutneys. Acids, especially from tomatoes, vinegar, and citrus juices, can eat into the metal thus contaminating the food. For best results, use nonreactive bowls made of stainless steel, porcelain, glass, or plastic.

Do not store garlic and other herbs in oil for more than 24 hours, even if refrigerated, unless they have been already acidified. Garlic can be acidified by marinating the peeled cloves in vinegar or citric acid for 12 hours; they can then be drained and stored in oil. However, garlic and other herbs can be stored safely in oil if the mixture contains an acid, such as vinegar, lemon or lime juice.

Tomatoes & Tomatillos

Tomatoes and tomatillos are used in many of the recipes in this book. When buying tomatoes, choose smooth, well-formed specimens that are firm (but not hard) and heavy for their size.

Tomatillos look like green cherry tomatoes enclosed in papery husks. Beneath the husk, you'll find a sticky-skinned fruit with an acidic flavor similar to that of green tomatoes. Tomatillos aren't usually served on their own; instead, they're cooked with other ingredients to make sauces and salsas. They also may be roasted separately, then added to a green chile salsa or other sauce.

To peel tomatoes, first dip in boiling water for 15 to 30 seconds, then plunge into cold water; pull skin off cooled tomatoes in strips.

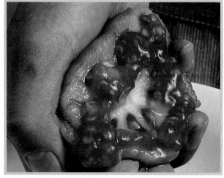

To seed tomatoes, cut in half lengthwise, then gently squeeze each half to remove seeds and juice; chop or slice tomatoes to use.

Chiles

Chiles differ in flavor and hotness depending on the type of pepper. Among the most familiar chiles, the mildest is the Anaheim (also called California, New Mexico, or Rio Grande green chile). Blackish green, heart-shaped pasilla (often confused with ancho or poblano) is mild to medium hot. Somewhat hotter are short, conical yellow wax peppers and jalapeño peppers.

Often, but not always, size indicates heat. Generally, smaller varieties are hotter than larger ones, because they have less flesh in proportion to the amount of veins.

Heat is concentrated in the interior veins or ribs near the seed heart—not in the seeds themselves, as is commonly believed. The seeds taste extra hot because they're in close contact with the veins.

Where the chiles are grown also affects their heat level. Those produced in cooler, wetter climates tend to be milder than those grown in hot, dry conditions.

If you make a sauce or salsa with mild chiles, and find it too mild, try adding a few pieces of a smaller hotter pepper variety, such as jalapeño or serrano.

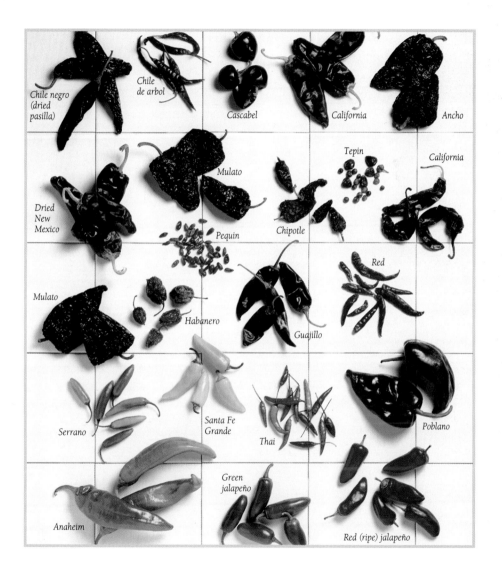

Chile negro (dried pasilla)

Chile de arbol

Cascabel

California

Ancho

Dried New Mexico

Mulato

Tepin

California

Pequin

Chipotle

Mulato

Habanero

Guajillo

Red

Serrano

Santa Fe Grande

Thai

Poblano

Anaheim

Green jalapeño

Red (ripe) jalapeño

Marinades

A marinade accomplishes several things. The acid (from citrus juice, wine, or vinegar) acts as a tenderizer. Fat (from olive oil, salad oil, or melted butter) adds moisture to very lean meat and fish. And seasonings impart interesting flavor. For best results, make the marinade in a heavy-duty plastic bag, nonreactive bowl, or pan. Let the food marinate for at least an hour—or, if possible, until the next day. Poultry and fish need not marinate as long. Turn meat, poultry, or fish several times while they're marinating.

Recipes

Honey-Wine Marinade

2 Tbsp. butter or margarine
1 cup dry white wine
2 Tbsp. white wine vinegar
⅓ cup honey
1 tsp. finely chopped fresh mint
    or crumbled dry mint
2 cloves garlic, minced or pressed

Melt butter over medium heat. Remove from heat and stir in remaining ingredients. Makes about 1½ cups.

Rosemary-Citrus Marinade

½ cup each orange, lemon,
    and lime juice
⅓ cup honey
¼ cup chopped onion
¼ cup olive oil or salad oil
2 Tbsp. Dijon mustard
2 tsp. fresh rosemary or 1 tsp. dry rosemary
½ tsp. each salt, ground coriander,
    and ground nutmeg
¼ tsp. pepper

In a bowl, combine ingredients. Makes about 2½ cups.

Basil-Parmesan Marinade

⅔ cup chopped fresh basil or 2 Tbsp.
    dry basil
¼ cup chopped parsley
¼ cup salad oil
⅓ cup white wine vinegar
3 Tbsp. grated Parmesan cheese
2 cloves garlic
⅛ tsp. pepper

In a blender or food processor, combine ingredients. Whirl until puréed. Makes about 1 cup.

Bastes

As a flavorful alternative to marinades, try brushing a basting sauce on food as it grills. The seasoning of a baste does not permeate as deeply as a marinade; the prime role of a baste is to conserve moisture in the food while it's grilling. To prevent scorching and flare-ups during cooking, do not apply basting sauces that are high in sugar or fat until the last few minutes of cooking.

Here are a few basting recipes to stimulate your creativity. Try matching up a baste with your favorite barbecue recipe.

Recipes

Parsley-Orange Baste

½ cup butter or margarine
2 Tbsp. grated orange zest
2 Tbsp. finely chopped parsley
2 Tbsp. honey
¼ cup lemon juice

Melt butter over medium heat; stir in zest, parsley, and honey. Remove from heat; stir in lemon juice. Makes about 1 cup.

Sesame-Soy Baste

⅓ cup soy sauce
3 Tbsp. each Oriental sesame oil and minced green onions
1 Tbsp. each vinegar and minced fresh ginger
2 tsp. sugar
2 cloves garlic, minced or pressed

Dash of ground red pepper (cayenne)
In a bowl, combine ingredients. Makes about 1 cup.

Mediterranean Baste

¼ cup butter or margarine
3 Tbsp. lemon juice
4 cloves garlic, minced or pressed
½ tsp. chopped fresh rosemary or oregano

Melt butter over medium heat; remove from heat; stir in lemon juice, garlic, and rosemary. Makes about ½ cup.

Lemon-Rosemary Baste

¼ cup butter or margarine
¼ cup lemon juice or dry sherry
¼ tsp. each dry rosemary and thyme

Melt butter over medium heat; remove from heat and stir in lemon juice, rosemary, and thyme. Makes about ½ cup.

Butters

Flavored butters make excellent basting sauces—just melt them, then brush over food as it cooks on the barbecue. Alternatively, you can bring butters to room temperature, then spoon them onto hot-from-the-grill meats, fish, or vegetables.

For best results, prepare and refrigerate butters at least one hour (or up to a week) in advance so that their flavors blend. Use the following recipes for butters to complement the smoky flavor of meat, fish, chicken, and vegetables cooked over charcoal.

Recipes

Ginger & Lime Butter

2-inch-long piece fresh ginger, minced
1 cup butter or margarine (softened)
1 tsp. coarsely ground pepper
¼ cup lime juice
1 tsp. grated lime zest

In a blender, combine ingredients and whirl until well blended. Makes about 1 cup.

Almond Browned Butter

¼ cup butter or margarine
¼ cup sliced almonds
2 Tbsp. lemon juice

Melt butter over medium heat. When butter foams, add almonds and stir until nuts begin to brown. Remove from heat; stir in lemon juice. Makes about ½ cup.

Dill Butter

½ cup butter or margarine (softened)
¼ cup chopped fresh dill

In a bowl, beat butter until fluffy; beat in dill. Makes about ¾ cup.

Nut Butter

¼ cup butter or margarine
½ chopped salted macadamia nuts or
    hazelnuts

Melt butter over medium heat; stir in nuts. Makes about ¾ cup.

Green Butter

½ cup butter or margarine (softened)
½ cup lightly packed fresh basil, mint,
    watercress, or parsley
1 tsp. lemon juice

In a blender, combine ingredients and whirl until well blended. Makes about ⅔ cup.

Rubs

Outdoor chefs will appreciate these aromatic blends for flavoring foods. Ginger, chiles, cilantro, and other herbs and spices add bold flavors. Though commonly called rubs, they are really thick pastes that are spread onto food before it is grilled.

Making a paste is easy; you simply grind the seasonings in a blender. To allow the flavors to permeate, refrigerate for at least 8 hours or until next day. Mix some of the reserved seasoning pastes with yogurt to make a cool sauce.

Recipes

Chile Paste

⅓ cup lemon juice
¼ cup salad oil
1 large onion, chopped
½ cup lightly packed cilantro
6 to 8 cloves garlic
1 Tbsp. chopped fresh ginger
1 or 2 fresh jalapeño chiles, seeded, stemmed

In a blender, combine ingredients and whirl until smoothly puréed. Makes about 1 cup.

Jamaican Jerk Paste

¾ cup coarsely chopped onion
4 cloves garlic, quartered
2 to 4 fresh jalapeño chiles, seeded, chopped
2 Tbsp. ground allspice
1 Tbsp. each minced fresh ginger and salad oil
1 tsp. each ground nutmeg and salt

In a blender, combine ingredients and whirl until puréed. Makes about ½ cup.

Escabeche Paste

8 cloves garlic, minced or pressed
1 tsp. each ground allspice, ground cloves, ground cumin, and ground coriander
1½ tsp. ground cinnamon
¾ tsp. coarsely ground pepper
2 tsp. dry oregano
¼ tsp. ground red pepper (cayenne)
2 Tbsp. each orange juice and white wine vinegar

Stir ingredients together. Makes about ¼ cup.

Peppercorn & Fennel Paste

2 Tbsp. whole black peppercorns
1 Tbsp. each fennel seed and rubbed dry sage

In a blender, whirl ingredients. Makes about ¼ cup.

SAUCES

*T*he rich flavors of sauces add another dimension to barbecued foods. Some of the recipes that follow are up-dated versions of traditional favorites; others are new and unusual combinations. What-ever your choice, use the sauces to dress up meats, fish, or vegetables sizzling hot from the grill.

Tomato-Raisin Sauce

(PICTURED ON PAGE 12)

*This spicy-sweet tomato-raisin sauce goes well
with chicken hot off the grill.*

◆

PER TABLESPOON: *25 calories, .30 g protein, 7 g carbohydrates, .03 g total fat, 0 mg cholesterol, 42 mg sodium*

PREPARATION TIME: *5 min.*

2 cloves garlic, minced
⅓ cup tomato sauce
1 Tbsp. firmly packed
   brown sugar
1 Tbsp. distilled white
   vinegar or cider vinegar
½ cup raisins

In a food processor or blender, whirl garlic, tomato sauce, sugar, vinegar, and raisins until raisins are chopped.

Makes about ¾ cup

Saffron Cream

Present grilled fish or shellfish in a pool of rich saffron cream.

◆

PER TABLESPOON: *24 calories, .28 g protein, .50 g carbohydrates, 2 g total fat, 8 mg cholesterol, 34 mg sodium*

PREPARATION TIME: *15 min.*

½ cup each *dry white wine
   and regular-strength
   chicken broth*
2 Tbsp. minced shallots
Pinch of ground saffron
½ cup whipping cream

In a 10- to 12-inch frying pan, combine wine, chicken broth, shallots, and saffron; bring to a boil; boil, uncovered, until reduced by half. Add cream, return to a boil, and boil until reduced to about 1 cup.

Makes about 1 cup

Chimichurri Sauce

Argentina's asado—a lavish barbecue meal
prepared by gauchos on the pampas—includes this
distinctive sauce to accompany grilled beef.

◆

PER TABLESPOON: 48 calories, .07 g protein, .68 g carbohydrates, 5 g total fat, 0 mg cholesterol, 2 mg sodium

PREPARATION TIME: *15 min.*

2 medium-size carrots,
    peeled
1 large firm-ripe tomato,
    cored
1 stalk celery
½ medium-size green bell
    pepper, stemmed, seeded
1 lemon, ends trimmed
1 clove garlic
½ tsp. each pepper and
    crushed dried hot red
    chiles
¼ cup each red wine
    and vinegar
¾ cup each olive oil and
    salad oil; or 1½ cups
    salad oil
Salt

Cut carrots, tomato, celery, bell pepper, and lemon into chunks. In a food processor, whirl vegetables and lemon chunks with garlic, a portion at a time, until very finely chopped; or chop very finely with a knife.

Mix chopped vegetable mixture, pepper, chiles, wine, vinegar, and oil. Season to taste with salt. Stir well before using.

Makes about 4 cups

Peanut Sauce

*S*erve this spicy,
mildly sweet peanut sauce with meat
or chicken kebabs.

◆

PER TABLESPOON: 36 calories, 2 g protein, 2 g carbohydrates, 3 g total fat, 0 mg cholesterol, 58 mg sodium

PREPARATION TIME: *10 min.*
COOKING TIME: *15 min.*

1 cup water
⅔ cup creamy peanut butter
2 cloves garlic, minced
   or pressed
2 Tbsp. firmly packed
   brown sugar
1½ Tbsp. lemon juice
1 Tbsp. soy sauce
¼ to ½ tsp. crushed red
   pepper flakes

In a 2-quart pan, combine water, peanut butter, and garlic. Cook over medium-low heat, stirring, until mixture boils and thickens. Remove from heat and stir in brown sugar, lemon juice, soy sauce, and crushed red pepper. Serve hot. If made ahead, cover and refrigerate for up to 2 days. To reheat, stir over low heat until hot; if necessary, add more water to restore to original consistency.

Makes about 2 cups

Smoky Chipotle Barbecue Sauce

*Smoked jalapeños give this sauce
its fiery flavor. Spoon it on spareribs or other
meats while they are grilling.*

◆

PER TABLESPOON: 20 calories, .20 g protein, 3 g carbohydrates, .98 g total fat, 0 mg cholesterol, 50 mg sodium

PREPARATION TIME: *10 min.*
COOKING TIME: *45 min.*

5 to 8 canned chipotle
   chiles in adobo sauce
3 Tbsp. salad oil
1 medium-size onion,
   chopped
2 cloves garlic, minced
   or pressed
1 large can (28 oz.)
   tomatoes
¼ cup each firmly packed
   brown sugar and red
   wine vinegar
Salt

Finely chop chiles in sauce; set aside.

Heat salad oil in a 3- to 4-quart pan over medium heat. Add onion and garlic. Cook, stirring occasionally, until onion is soft (about 10 minutes). Stir in tomatoes, brown sugar, vinegar, and chiles. Break up tomatoes with a spoon, then cover and cook, stirring occasionally until sauce is thickened and smooth (about 30 minutes). Season to taste with salt.

Makes about 3 cups

Ginger-Lemon Sauce

Made with fresh ginger, lemon zest, and
whipping cream, this versatile sauce dresses up grilled fish,
skewered scallops, or shrimp.

◆

PER TABLESPOON: 49 calories, .31 g protein, .51 g carbohydrates, 5 g total fat, 16 mg cholesterol, 34 mg sodium

PREPARATION TIME: *10 min.*
COOKING TIME: *15 min.*

½ *cup each dry white wine
and regular-strength
chicken broth*
2 *Tbsp. finely chopped
shallots*
1 *tsp. grated fresh ginger*
¼ *tsp. grated lemon zest*
½ *cup whipping cream*
¼ *cup unsalted butter*

In a wide frying pan, combine wine, chicken broth, shallots, ginger, and lemon zest. Bring to a boil over high heat; boil uncovered until reduced by about half.

Add cream, return to a boil, and boil until mixture is reduced to ¾ cup.

Reduce heat to low. Add butter in one piece; stir with a whisk until butter is melted and smoothly blended into sauce.

To keep sauce warm for up to 4 hours, pour into top of a double boiler or into a measuring cup, then set in water that is just hot to the touch. Stir sauce occasionally, replacing hot water as needed. Do not reheat or sauce will separate.

Makes about 1 cup

Blackberry Sauce

This burgundy-colored sauce is
tart-sweet and slightly hot. Pour it over grilled pork,
lamb, chicken, or fish.

◆

PER TABLESPOON: *57 calories, .20 g protein, 15 g carbohydrates, .11 g total fat, 0 mg cholesterol, 2 mg sodium*

PREPARATION TIME: *15 min.*
COOKING TIME: *1 hr. 30 min.*

8 *cups blackberries, rinsed,
    drained*
1¾ *cups red wine vinegar*
1 *cup firmly packed brown
    sugar*
1 *cup granulated sugar*
2 *tsp. ground cinnamon*
1½ *tsp. ground allspice*
1 *tsp. ground ginger*
½ *tsp. pepper*
¼ *tsp. ground red pepper
    (cayenne)*

In a 4- to 5-quart pan, stir berries often over medium-high heat until they become juicy and begin to fall apart (about 10 minutes). Rub berries and juice through a fine strainer into a bowl; discard seeds.

Return berry juice to pan and add vinegar, brown sugar, granulated sugar, cinnamon, allspice, ginger, pepper, and ground red pepper. Bring mixture to a boil over high heat; simmer gently, uncovered and stirring often, until berry sauce is reduced to 2½ cups (about 1 hour).

Cool sauce before serving.

Makes about 2½ cups

Classic Barbecue Sauce

Spicy and sweet, this red sauce makes a great
glaze for beef, chicken, or ribs; one cup is enough
to baste about three pounds of meat.

◆

PER TABLESPOON: *18 calories, .21 g protein, 4 g carbohydrates, .26 g total fat, 0 mg cholesterol, 90 mg sodium*

PREPARATION TIME: *10 min.*
COOKING TIME: *1 hr. 30 min.*

3 medium-size (about 1 lb.
 total) onions, chopped
3 cloves garlic, minced
 or pressed
1 Tbsp. salad oil
2 cups catsup
1 cup each cider vinegar
 and dry red wine
⅓ cup firmly packed
 brown sugar
1 Tbsp. dry mustard
1 tsp. ground ginger
½ tsp. each ground red
 pepper (cayenne) and
 pepper

In a 5- to 6-quart pan over medium-high heat, mix
onions, garlic, and oil. Cook, stirring often, until
onions are limp (about 10 minutes).

   Add catsup, vinegar, wine, brown sugar, dry mustard, ground ginger, ground red pepper, and pepper.
Stirring, bring to a boil on high heat. Reduce heat to
medium-low and simmer, uncovered, stirring occasionally until sauce is reduced to 4 cups (about 1½
hours). Serve sauce warm or at room temperature.

Makes about 4 cups

Southwest Barbecue Sauce

Brush this smoky all-purpose
sauce on chicken or beef while it's still
sizzling on the grill.

◆

PER TABLESPOON: *14 calories, .21 g protein, 3 g carbohydrates, .37 g total fat, 0 mg cholesterol, 82 mg sodium*

PREPARATION TIME: *10 min.*
COOKING TIME: *30 min.*

2 Tbsp. salad oil
1 medium-size onion,
  chopped
1 large clove garlic,
  minced or pressed
1 large can (28 oz.)
  tomato purée
½ cup firmly packed
  brown sugar
¼ cup cider vinegar
3 Tbsp. Worcestershire
  sauce
2 tsp. liquid smoke
1 tsp. dry mustard
4 to 6 tsp. ground dried
  New Mexico chile
1 to 1½ tsp. salt

Heat salad oil in a 3- to 4-quart pan over medium heat. Add onion and garlic; cook, stirring occasionally, until onion is soft (about 10 minutes). Stir in tomato purée, brown sugar, vinegar, Worcestershire sauce, liquid smoke, and dry mustard. Then add ground New Mexico chile and salt. Bring to a boil over high heat, then reduce heat. Cover and simmer for 20 minutes to blend flavors.

Makes about 5 cups

Shiitake Sauce

*The mild flavor of fresh shiitake
mushrooms enriches this simple sauce; serve it
with grilled flank steak.*

◆

PER TABLESPOON: *10 calories, .37 g protein, .66 g carbohydrates, .67 g total fat, 0 mg cholesterol, 62 mg sodium*

PREPARATION TIME: *10 min.*
COOKING TIME: *30 min.*

1 lb. fresh shiitake
   mushrooms, minced
2 *Tbsp. salad oil*
2 *Tbsp. minced fresh ginger*
3 *cups regular-strength
   chicken or beef broth*
1 *Tbsp. cornstarch*

Cut off and discard tough stems from mushrooms. Rinse and drain caps, then cut into ¼-inch-wide strips. In a 10- to 12-inch frying pan, combine mushrooms, salad oil, and ginger; stir often on medium-high heat until mushrooms are lightly browned (about 10 minutes).

Pour broth into pan. Boil, stirring often, on high heat until sauce is reduced to 2 cups (15 to 20 minutes). Dissolve cornstarch with a little of the broth; stir into pan. Stir on high heat until boiling.

Makes about 3 cups

SAUCES & SALSAS FOR THE GRILL

Cabernet-Cherry Sauce

*This festive sauce, made with
dried tart cherries and Cabernet Sauvignon,
is delicious with grilled beef.*

◆

PER TABLESPOON: *9 calories, .03 g protein, 2 g carbohydrates, .01 g total fat, 0 mg cholesterol, 44 mg sodium*

PREPARATION TIME: *10 min.*

3 cups beef broth
1½ cups Cabernet Sauvignon
1½ cups dried tart cherries,
   such as Montmorency
2½ Tbsp. red current jelly
2 Tbsp. cornstarch mixed
   with ¼ cup water

In a 3- to 4-quart pan, combine 3 cups broth, wine, cherries, and jelly; bring to a boil over high heat. Cover and simmer over low heat until cherries soften (15 to 20 minutes).

Bring broth mixture to a boil. Add cornstarch mixture, and stir until sauce boils. Pour into a serving bowl.

Makes about 6½ cups

Lemon-Herb Mayonnaise

*S*erve this zippy mayonnaise
with slices of turkey breast, sizzling hot
off the grill.

◆

PER TABLESPOON: *99 calories, .15 g protein, .42 g carbohydrates, 11 g total fat, 8 mg cholesterol, 78 mg sodium*

PREPARATION TIME: *10 min.*

½ cup mayonnaise
1 Tbsp. minced fresh
marjoram
½ tsp. grated lemon zest

Mix together mayonnaise, marjoram, and grated lemon zest.

Makes about ½ cup

Green Mayonnaise

*W*atercress, spinach, and parsley add color and flavor to prepared mayonnaise.

◆

PER TABLESPOON: *63 calories, .24 g protein, .11 g carbohydrates, 7 g total fat, 7 mg cholesterol, 7 mg sodium*

PREPARATION TIME: *15 min.*

8 watercress sprigs
6 to 10 spinach leaves
5 parsley sprigs
1½ cups prepared
mayonnaise
2 tsp. lemon juice

In a bowl, combine watercress sprigs, spinach leaves, and parsley sprigs. Cover with boiling water and let stand for about 5 minutes. Drain, rinse with cold water, and drain again, pressing out excess moisture.

In a blender or food processor, combine prepared mayonnaise, greens, and lemon juice.

Makes about 2 cups

Curried Coconut
Cream Sauce

*Inspired by Hawaiian cuisine, this
creamy sauce adds another dimension to grilled
chicken or shrimp skewers.*

◆

PER TABLESPOON: 42 calories, .43 g protein, 2 g carbohydrates, 4 g total fat, 2 mg cholesterol, 10 mg sodium

PREPARATION TIME: *10 min.*
COOKING TIME: *45 min.*

6 Tbsp. butter or margarine
3 large onions, chopped
3 cloves garlic, minced
   or pressed
2 Tbsp. minced fresh ginger
¼ cup all-purpose flour
3 Tbsp. curry powder
1 Tbsp. sugar
½ tsp. crushed red pepper
   flakes
4 cans (12 to 14 oz. each)
   unsweetened coconut milk,
   thawed if frozen or 6 cups
   half-and-half or light
   cream mixed with 1 Tbsp.
   each sugar and coconut
   extract
Salt

Melt butter in a wide frying pan over medium-high
heat. Add onions, garlic, and ginger. Cook, stirring occasionally, until onions are soft (about 15
minutes). Stir in flour, curry powder, sugar, and red
pepper. Cook, stirring occasionally, until hot and
bubbly. Remove from heat and smoothly blend
in coconut milk.

Bring sauce to a boil over medium heat, stirring
frequently. Continue to cook, uncovered, stirring
frequently, until sauce is reduced to about 6 cups
(15 to 20 minutes). Season to taste with salt.

Makes about 6 cups

California Catsup

*Tomatoes—spiced with garlic, coriander,
ground red pepper, nutmeg, and cinnamon—combine to
make a tangy sauce for grilled meats.*

◆

PER TABLESPOON: 23 calories, .37 g protein, 6 g carbohydrates, .12 g total fat, 0 mg cholesterol, 47 mg sodium

PREPARATION TIME: *15 min.*
COOKING TIME: *2 hrs.*

6 *lb. ripe Roma-type
    tomatoes, cored, chopped*
1 *large onion, chopped*
2 *Tbsp. chopped garlic*
1½ *cups cider vinegar*
1 *cup sugar*
1 *tsp. ground coriander*
½ *to ¾ tsp. ground red
    pepper (cayenne)*
½ *tsp. ground mace or
    nutmeg*
¼ *tsp. ground cinnamon*
1 *dry bay leaf*
About 1¼ tsp. salt

In a blender or food processor, combine tomatoes,
onion, and garlic, a portion at a time, and whirl
until smoothly puréed. Pour mixture through a fine
strainer set over a 5- to 6-quart pan, stirring and
pressing to push mixture through. Discard any
residue left in strainer. To pan, add vinegar, sugar,
coriander, ground red pepper, mace, cinnamon,
and bay leaf.

Boil gently, uncovered and stirring often, until
mixture is thick and reduced to about 4 cups, 1½
to 2 hours (adjust heat to maintain a gentle boil;
if mixture splatters out of pan, lower heat). Add salt
to taste. Remove and discard bay leaf. Serve warm
or cool.

Makes about 4 cups

Lime Sauce

*F*reshly squeezed lime juice adds the sparkle
and a green chile pepper imparts the heat; serve the sauce
with grilled fish or seafood.

◆

PER TABLESPOON: 7 calories, .52 g protein, 2 g carbohydrates, .01 g total fat, 0 mg cholesterol, 516 mg sodium

PREPARATION TIME: 5 min.

3 Tbsp. each soy sauce
  and lime juice
1 fresh small hot green chile
  (such as jalapeño or
  serrano), seeded, minced

In a small bowl, mix together soy sauce, lime
juice, and chile.

Makes about ¼ cup

Ginger-Hoisin Sauce

*B*aste chicken with this elegant sauce during the last 10 minutes or so of grilling.

◆

PER TABLESPOON: 32 calories, .47 g protein, 4 g carbohydrates, .94 g total fat, 0 mg cholesterol, 342 mg sodium

PREPARATION TIME: 5 min.

⅔ cup hoisin sauce
⅓ cup dry sherry or water
2 Tbsp. chopped fresh ginger
4 cloves garlic, minced or
  pressed
1 Tbsp. sesame oil

In a bowl, stir together hoisin sauce, sherry,
ginger, garlic, and sesame oil.

Makes about 1 cup

SALSAS

Tomatoes, tomatillos, and fruit combine with vinegar, citrus juice, chiles, onions, garlic, and cilantro to make up many of the recipes in this section. Some salsas are brushed onto food before it is grilled; others are best served as a condiment with the finished dish.

Salsa Fresca

(PICTURED ON PAGE 36)

Made in a blender, this quintessential Mexican condiment
has a moist consistency. For a chunkier texture, make it by hand.

◆

PER TABLESPOON: 12 calories, .15 g protein, 1 g carbohydrates, .89 g total fat, 0 mg cholesterol, 1 mg sodium

PREPARATION TIME: *10 min.*

2 *cloves garlic*
½ *medium-size onion,*
   quartered
1 *to 2 jalapeño or other*
   small hot chiles, stemmed,
   seeded
¼ *cup packed cilantro*
1 *lb. firm-ripe tomatoes,*
   seeded, coarsely chopped
2 *Tbsp. salad oil*
Juice of 1 lime
Salt and pepper

In a blender or food processor, combine garlic, onion, chiles, cilantro, and tomatoes; whirl briefly just until coarsely chopped. Add oil and lime juice; whirl until mixture is finely chopped. Season to taste with salt and pepper.

If making by hand, use a sharp knife to mince garlic, onion, and chiles. Finely chop cilantro and dice tomatoes. Combine in a nonreactive bowl; then add oil and lime juice. Season to taste with salt and pepper, if desired.

Makes 2 cups

Smoky Roasted Salsa

*Roasting the ingredients in a dry frying pan gives
this spicy salsa an extraordinary flavor; a chipotle chile adds heat
and smokiness. Serve with meats or sausages.*

◆

PER TABLESPOON: 10 calories, .17 g protein, 1 g carbohydrates, .61 g total fat, 0 mg cholesterol, 5 mg sodium

PREPARATION TIME: *10 min.*
COOKING TIME: *10 min.*

3 *cloves garlic, peeled*
1 *medium-size onion,*
  quartered
3 *large tomatoes*
1 *canned chipotle chile in*
  adobo sauce
¼ *cup lime juice*
2 *Tbsp. salad oil*
¼ *cup packed cilantro*

Place a 10- to 12-inch uncoated frying pan over high
heat. Add garlic, onion, and tomatoes. Cook, turn-
ing often with tongs, until charred on all sides
(about 10 minutes). Remove from pan and let cool.
Cut tomatoes in half crosswise and discard seeds.

In a blender or food processor, combine vegetables, chipotle, lime juice, oil, and cilantro; whirl to
desired consistency (either chunky or smooth).

Makes 3 cups

Roasted Tomatillo Salsa

Green tomatillos, pan-roasted
with chiles and onions, make a pleasingly tart salsa.
Cilantro and lime season the mix.

◆

PER TABLESPOON: *5 calories, .22 g protein, 1 g carbohydrates, .04 g total fat, 0 mg cholesterol, .60 mg sodium*

PREPARATION TIME: *20 min.*
COOKING TIME: *15 min.*

¾ lb. tomatillos
¼ lb. small (about 1 inch
 wide) onions
1 or 2 (about ¼ lb. total)
 mild fresh green chiles
 such as poblano or
 Anaheim
½ cup packed cilantro
2 to 4 Tbsp. lime juice
Salt

Pull off and discard tomatillo husks. Rinse tomatillos and set aside 1 tomatillo that is about 1½ inches wide. Place remaining tomatillos, onions (don't peel onions if you want sauce to have a mild roasted flavor), and chile in a 10- to 12-inch frying pan over high heat (use an old pan; the process tends to discolor the surface). Shake pan or turn vegetables frequently until they are charred all over (about 15 minutes).

Tomatillos should be soft when pressed. Let vegetables cool. Peel onions if roasted in their skins. Pull loose skin from chile and discard; also cut out and discard stem and seed.

In a food processor or with a knife, mince uncooked tomatillo, roasted tomatillos, onions, chile, and cilantro. Season mixture to taste with lime juice and salt.

Makes about 2 cups

Red & Yellow Pepper Salsa

*Show off the season's
best bell peppers in this nutritious salsa.
Serve it with grilled fish or chicken.*

◆

PER TABLESPOON: *4 calories, .09 g protein, .87 g carbohydrates, .01 g total fat, 0 mg cholesterol, .28 mg sodium*

PREPARATION TIME: *15 min.*

2 *large yellow bell peppers
    (about 1 lb. total), seeded,
    diced*
1 *large red bell pepper
    (about 8 oz.), seeded,
    diced*
⅔ *cup peeled, minced jicama*
2 *Tbsp. minced cilantro*
1½ *Tbsp. distilled white
    vinegar*
1 *tsp. honey*
*About ⅛ tsp. ground red
    pepper (cayenne), or
    to taste*

In a nonreactive bowl, combine yellow bell pepper, red bell pepper, jicama, cilantro, vinegar, honey, and ground red pepper; mix gently.

Makes about 2 cups

Banana Salsa

Bananas, raisins, cilantro, and lemongrass
combine to make an exotic-tasting condiment. Serve it
with grilled Hawaiian fish.

◆

PER TABLESPOON: *25 calories, .24 g protein, 6 g carbohydrates, .34 g total fat, 0 mg cholesterol, .66 mg sodium*

PREPARATION TIME: *10 min.*
COOKING TIME: *8 min.*

1 large (½ lb.) firm-ripe
  banana
1 tsp. Oriental sesame oil
½ cup chopped golden
  raisins
2 Tbsp. chopped cilantro
2 Tbsp. minced fresh
  lemongrass (tender part
  only) or 1 tsp. grated
  lemon zest
1 tsp. Japanese chile spice
  (nanami togarashi) or
  ¼ tsp. ground red pepper
  (cayenne) and ½ tsp.
  grated orange zest

Peel and halve banana lengthwise. In a nonstick 10-
to 12-inch frying pan over high heat, brown banana
well in Oriental sesame oil (about 8 minutes).

Coarsely chop banana. Mix with raisins,
cilantro, lemongrass, and Japanese chile spice.

Makes about 1 cup

Cilantro-Lime Salsa

*Cool and refreshing,
here's a summertime salsa that is especially
delicious with grilled shellfish.*

◆

PER TABLESPOON: 26 calories, .04 g protein, .57 g carbohydrates, 3 g total fat, 0 mg cholesterol, .89 mg sodium

PREPARATION TIME: *10 min.*

1 *small onion, finely chopped*
1 *cup chopped cilantro*
½ *cup each chopped parsley
   and salad oil*
6 *Tbsp. lime juice*
3 *Tbsp. distilled white
   vinegar*
2 *cloves garlic, minced
   or pressed*
1 *jalapeño or other small
   hot chile, stemmed,
   seeded, minced*

In a nonreactive bowl, mix onion, cilantro, parsley, oil, lime juice, vinegar, garlic, and chile.

Makes about 2½ cups

Cranberry Salsa

*Serve this salsa
with grilled turkey or other poultry,
lamb, or pork dishes.*

◆

PER TABLESPOON: 17 calories, .06 g protein, 2 g carbohydrates, 1 g total fat, 0 mg cholesterol, .09 mg sodium

PREPARATION TIME: *15 min.*

2 *large oranges*
2 *cups fresh cranberries*
1 *fresh jalapeño or other
   small hot chile*
4 *tsp. grated orange zest*
¼ *cup each minced onion
   and salad oil*
1 *Tbsp. each minced
   cilantro and fresh ginger*
Salt

Cut peel and white membrane from oranges; lift out sections and coarsely chop. Using a knife or a food processor, coarsely chop cranberries. Stem, seed, and mince the chile.

In a nonreactive bowl, combine oranges, cranberries, chile, orange zest, onion, salad oil, cilantro, and ginger. Mix thoroughly, then season to taste with salt.

Makes about 3 cups

Lime Salsa

Tomatillos and fresh lime make a marvelously tart salsa.
Look for firm, smooth tomatillos; before using them, remove the papery husks
and rinse off the sticky coating.

◆

PER TABLESPOON: 2 calories, .07 g protein, .34 g carbohydrates, .02 g total fat, 0 mg cholesterol, .37 mg sodium

PREPARATION TIME: *15 min.*

1 *large, ripe red or yellow*
   tomato (about 8 oz.),
   finely diced
8 *medium-size tomatillos*
   (about 8 oz. total),
   husked, rinsed, chopped
¼ *cup minced red or yellow*
   bell pepper
2 *Tbsp. minced red onion*
1 *tsp. grated lime zest*
1 *Tbsp. lime juice*

In a nonreactive bowl, mix tomato, tomatillos, bell pepper, onion, lime zest, and lime juice.

Makes about 4 cups

Peach & Honeydew Salsa

*Juicy peaches and honeydew in tiny cubes,
sparked by mint, tarragon, lemon, and rice vinegar, make
a new-wave salsa for grilled fish.*

◆

PER TABLESPOON: *5 calories, .05 g protein, 1 g carbohydrates, 0 g total fat, 0 mg cholesterol, 13 mg sodium*

PREPARATION TIME: *10 min.*

1½ cups ¼-inch-dice
   honeydew melon
1½ cups ¼-inch-dice peeled
   firm-ripe peaches
2 Tbsp. seasoned rice
   vinegar or 2 Tbsp. rice
   vinegar with ½ tsp. sugar
2 Tbsp. minced fresh mint
1 Tbsp. lemon juice
1 Tbsp. minced fresh or
   ½ tsp. dried tarragon
Salt

In a nonreactive bowl, gently mix together melon, peaches, vinegar, mint, lemon juice, and tarragon; add salt to taste.

Makes about 3 cups

RELISHES & CHUTNEYS

*R*elishes are piquant blends
of vegetables, fruits, spices,
and vinegar. Their flavors,
ranging from hot and spicy to
mild and tangy, provide the
finishing touch to grilled foods.
Chutneys are a type of relish,
too. Though usually associated
with Eastern or Indian food,
try serving them with a variety of foods from the grill.

Cranberry Relish

(PICTURED ON PAGE 52)

Crimson cranberry relish gets its tender crunch from water chestnuts; cilantro and Dijon mustard add intriguing nuances to this holiday favorite.

◆

PER TABLESPOON: *16 calories, .10 g protein, 4 g carbohydrates, .05 g total fat, 0 mg cholesterol, 15 mg sodium*

PREPARATION TIME: *5 min.*

1 bag (12 oz. or 3 cups) cranberries, rinsed, drained
1 can (8 oz.) water chestnuts, drained
1 cup lightly packed cilantro
1 Tbsp. Dijon mustard
¼ to ⅓ cup sugar

In a food processor (or a food chopper with coarse blade), coarsely chop cranberries, water chestnuts, and cilantro. Stir in mustard and sugar to taste.

Makes about 2 cups

Pomegranate-Orange Relish

*The colors and tastes of
pomegranate seeds and blood oranges blend
harmoniously in this lively relish.*

◆

PER TABLESPOON: *11 calories, .16 g protein, 3 g carbohydrates, .02 g total fat, 0 mg cholesterol, .70 mg sodium*

PREPARATION TIME: *30 min.*

1 cup coarsely chopped
  red onion
4 *cups ice cubes*
2 *cups water*
¼ *cup raspberry or red
  wine vinegar*
2 *medium-size (about 1 lb.
  total) pomegranates*
4 *or 5 medium-size (about
  1¼ lb. total) blood or
  common oranges*
¼ *cup red wine vinegar*
4 *tsp. sugar*
2 *tsp. prepared horseradish*
Salt

Put red onions in a bowl with water to cover.
Squeeze onions to bruise lightly; drain. Add ice
cubes, water, and vinegar. Let stand until crisp
(20 to 30 minutes).

Meanwhile, score sides of pomegranates with a
sharp knife. Holding fruit under water in a large
bowl, separate into large chunks. With your fingers,
separate seeds from membrane and skin. Skim off
membrane and skin; pour out water and drain seeds.

Finely shred 1 to 2 teaspoons zest from orange;
set aside. With a sharp knife, cut zest and white
membrane from oranges. Holding oranges over a
bowl to catch the juice, cut between the inner membranes to free segments. Squeeze juice from membranes into bowl; discard membranes. Gently mix
fruit with the vinegar, sugar, and horseradish; pour
mixture into a shallow nonreactive bowl.

Drain onions. Sprinkle orange mixture with pomegranate seeds and crisped onions. Add salt to taste.

Makes about 3 cups

Spicy Pepper Relish

*This colorful relish of red
and yellow bell peppers and hot chiles beautifully
complements grilled lamb.*

◆

PER TABLESPOON: 42 calories, .3 g protein, 10 g carbohydrates, .15 g total fat, 0 mg cholesterol, 1 mg sodium

PREPARATION TIME: *5 min.*
COOKING TIME: *30 min.*

2 large each *(about 2 lb.
   total) red and yellow
   bell peppers*
8 *(about 3 oz. total) red or
   green serrano chiles*
1 *cup sugar*
⅔ *cup distilled white vinegar*

Stem, seed, and cut red and yellow peppers and chiles into fine strips. Mix with sugar and vinegar.

In a 10- to 12-inch frying pan over medium heat, cook pepper mixture, uncovered; stir often until most of the liquid evaporates (about 30 minutes). Cool.

Makes about 1½ cups

Papaya-Plum Chutney

*Colorful papayas and red plums combine with
raisins and sweet spices in an exotic-tasting chutney.
It goes well with game or poultry.*

◆

PER TABLESPOON: *26 calories, .12 g protein, 7 g carbohydrates, .05 g total fat, 0 mg cholesterol, 24 mg sodium*

PREPARATION TIME: *15 min.*
COOKING TIME: *1 hr.*

1¼ cups cider vinegar
1¾ cups sugar
½ cup golden raisins
2 cloves garlic, minced
 or pressed
3 Tbsp. chopped
 crystallized ginger
1 cinnamon stick
 (about 3 inches long)
1 tsp. salt
⅛ to ¼ tsp. ground red
 pepper (cayenne)
2 medium-size ripe papayas
 (about 1 lb. each)
2 lb. red plums

In a heavy-bottomed 8- to 10-quart pan, mix vinegar, sugar, raisins, garlic, ginger, cinnamon stick, salt, and red pepper. Bring to a boil over high heat, stirring often. Reduce heat to medium-low and simmer, uncovered, stirring occasionally to prevent sticking, until syrup is slightly thickened (about 15 minutes).

Peel and halve papayas; scoop out seeds. Cut fruit into ½-inch chunks. Pit and quarter plums. Add papayas and plums to syrup and continue to simmer, uncovered, stirring occasionally, until papaya is tender when pierced and chutney is thickened (about 35 minutes). Discard cinnamon stick.

Makes about 6 cups

Tomato-Lemon Chutney

*A sauce for sausages, this
condiment adds just the right flourish to a platter
of grilled bratwurst or kielbasa.*

◆

PER TABLESPOON: 32 calories, .36 g protein, 7 g carbohydrates, .65 g total fat, 0 mg cholesterol, 27 mg sodium

PREPARATION TIME: *10 min.*
COOKING TIME: *20 min.*

1 or 2 lemons
1 can (about 1 lb.) tomatoes
1 Tbsp. salad oil or olive oil
1 small dried hot red chile
1 Tbsp. mustard seeds
½ tsp. cumin seeds
¼ tsp. ground nutmeg
*½ cup each raisins
    and sugar*

Grate enough lemon zest to make 2 teaspoons;
set aside.

Using a sharp knife, cut peel and all white membrane from one lemon. In a blender, whirl lemon
with tomatoes and their liquid just until blended.

In a 1½- to 2-quart pan, combine oil, chile,
lemon zest, mustard seeds, cumin seeds, and nutmeg. Cook over medium-high heat, stirring, until
seeds begin to pop. Add tomato mixture, raisins,
and sugar.

Boil gently, uncovered, until mixture thickens to
a jamlike consistency (about 20 minutes); stir often.

Makes about 1¾ cups

Refrigerator Corn Relish

A *quick refrigerator version of an old-fashioned favorite, this colorful relish is a popular accompaniment to frankfurters, hamburgers, or other meats.*

◆

PER TABLESPOON: *14 calories, .30 g protein, 3 g carbohydrates, .11 g total fat, 0 mg cholesterol, 45 mg sodium*

PREPARATION TIME: *20 min.*
COOKING TIME: *10 min.*

1¼ *cups distilled white vinegar*
¾ *cup sugar*
2½ *tsp. salt*
1¼ *tsp. celery seeds*
¾ *tsp. mustard seeds*
½ *tsp. liquid hot pepper seasoning*
8 *cups fresh corn kernels (cut from about 10 large ears of corn)*
1 *each small green and red bell pepper, seeded, chopped*
3 *green onions, thinly sliced*

In a heavy-bottomed 8- to 10-quart pan, mix vinegar, sugar, salt, celery seeds, mustard seeds, hot pepper seasoning, and corn. Bring to a simmer over medium heat; simmer, uncovered for 5 minutes. Remove from heat and let cool.

Stir bell peppers and onions into corn mixture.

Makes about 8 cups

Pineapple, Ginger & Orange Chutney

*Spoon this ginger-flavored
chutney of orange and pineapple chunks
onto grilled steak.*

◆

PER TABLESPOON: 12 calories, .06 g protein, 3 g carbohydrates, .03 g total fat, 0 mg cholesterol, .16 mg sodium

PREPARATION TIME: *20 min.*
COOKING TIME: *1 hr.*

2 *medium-size (about 1 lb.)*
   oranges
⅓ *cup minced fresh ginger*
⅓ *cup sugar*
1½ *cups ½-inch chunks*
   pineapple
¾ *cup seeded, chopped*
   thin-skinned European
   cucumber

With a vegetable peeler, pare zest from oranges, and cut it into long, very thin slivers. Cut off and discard remaining peel and white membrane from each orange. Holding fruit over a nonreactive bowl, cut parallel to membrane to release segments. Squeeze juice into bowl; discard membrane.

In a 1½- to 2-quart pan, combine zest and ginger. Add 2 cups water and bring to a boil, uncovered, over high heat; drain. Add 2 cups more water and repeat.

To the zest and ginger, add orange juice drained from fruit, 1 cup water, and sugar. Bring to a boil on high heat and cook uncovered, stirring occasionally, until liquid has almost cooked away (about 10 minutes); avoid scorching. Meanwhile, add pineapple and cucumber to orange segments.

When boiling syrup is reduced (fruit zest should look translucent), stir in 2 tablespoons water to thin the mixture, then pour over fruit. Mix gently. Serve warm or at room temperature.

Makes about 3 cups

Mango-Apricot-Date Chutney

*In this easy chutney, we used dried mangoes
from an Asian market. You'll also find
the preserved or pickled ginger at such a store.*

◆

PER TABLESPOON: *43 calories, .28 g protein, 11 g carbohydrates, .05 g total fat, 0 mg cholesterol, 4 mg sodium*

PREPARATION TIME: *15 min.*
COOKING TIME: *1 hr. 15 min.*

3½ cups water
*½ lb. each dried mangoes
  and dried apricots; or
  1 lb. dried apricots*
*¾ cup each golden raisins
  and currants*
*1¼ cups pitted dates,
  coarsely snipped
  or chopped*
1½ cups white wine vinegar
*1¼ cups firmly packed
  brown sugar*
*1 cup preserved ginger in
  syrup or pickled ginger,
  drained, coarsely chopped*
1 Tbsp. mustard seeds
1½ tsp. chili powder
Salt

In a 5- to 6-quart pan, combine water and mangoes.
Bring to a simmer, cover, and cook for 5 minutes.
Add apricots and continue to simmer, covered, for 5
more minutes. (If using all apricots, simmer for only
5 minutes total.) Add raisins, currants, dates, vinegar, sugar, ginger, mustard seeds, and chili powder.
Simmer, uncovered, stirring more frequently as mixture thickens, until most of the liquid has evaporat-
ed and chutney is thick (45 minutes to 1 hour).
Season to taste with salt.

Makes about 6 cups

Index